The Holistic Overcomer Mindset Guide

By

Nichol Ellis-McGregor

No part of this publication may be reproduced, stored, or transmitted in any form or by any means, electronic, mechanical, photocopying, recording, scanning, or otherwise, except as permitted under Section 107 or 108 of the 1976 United States Copyright Act without the prior written permission of the author. Requests to the author or publisher for permission should be addressed to the following email.

Limit of liability/disclaimer of warranty:
While the publisher and author have used their best efforts in preparing this guide, they make no representation or warranties with respect to the accuracy or completeness of the contents of this document and specifically disclaim any implied warranties of merchantability or fitness for particular purpose. No warranty may be created or extended by sales representatives, promoters, or written sales materials.
The advice and strategies contained herein may not be suitable for your situation. You should consult with a professional where appropriate.

Neither the publisher nor the author shall be liable for any loss of profit or any other commercial damages, including but not limited to special, incidental, consequential, or other damages.
Copyright© 2021

Unless otherwise indicated, all scripture quotations are taken from the King James Version (KJV), Passion Translation, NIV or the Message Translation of the Holy Bible.

Acknowledgements

I like to thank my Lord and Savior Jesus Christ, my husband, children, family and supporters that encouraged me on my journey.

    I dedicate this book to my late brother Caine. The loss of you inspired me to write this book.

Table of Contents

Introduction 1

Chapter 1: Unique 11

Chapter 2: His Image 20

Chapter 3: Different 43

Chapter 4: Fear 58

Chapter 5: Grace 67

Chapter 6: Wellness 76

Chapter 7: Reset 79

Chapter 8: Serve 90

Chapter 9: Legacy 93

Conclusion 97

Introduction

You were born for such a time of this! No matter your background, circumstances, situations, or conditions. Being born in unique, dire, unprepared and unstable conditions does not keep you from being complete, or whole. You are not forgotten! However, your circumstances can prepare you for your purpose, destiny, drive and God's perfect will for your life.

Think about Jesus who was not born into the best conditions. He was born in a manger with animals. They most likely didn't smell the best. I don't care about the conditions of your birth lineage. It doesn't matter if it was in wedlock, out of wedlock, foster care, one parent, two parents, or no parents in your home or if you were rejected. Your life was designed for a purpose. Even if your parent(s) abandoned you or left you in a shameful condition: you are here! YOU ARE NOT A MISTAKE! You are a living, breathing human being. You were born with a purpose! You have beaten the odds! "Scientists estimate the probability of your very existence, being born, is at about one in 400 trillion!" (TEDTALKS). YOU ARE A MIRACLE!

The chances of you being born are a miracle. People who experience rejection and trauma need to know their life is filled with purpose and meaning.

They need to know that being born out of wedlock, in a particular zip code and in shame does not define you or your destiny!

Some people accepted me but there were some who did not. On the maternal side of my family, I was different. I was different as I didn't want to replicate the trauma and dysfunction. This made me a target as to *who is this girl? Where does she come from? And who does she think she is?* Rejection and isolation can come from your own family. This is not set up to destroy you but to build you. This issue does not exempt anyone from experiencing this.

Even some accomplished, successful and famous people have been scarred from negative experiences or a parent (or parent's) abandoning them. I want people to know that although those conditions happened, you are destined to be here! Many are dealing with these dynamics and influences that challenge them in certain areas. However, God can walk us through disturbing experiences so God can elevate us to where we are truly destined to be.

A young lady shared with me that she deals with fear and rejection. It's okay. We all have to deal with it even if we are successful. There may be times when we encounter someone who causes us to revisit those feelings. We must strive to overcome trauma by creating boundaries. We must also focus on our healing and wellness and creating a supportive village.

A supportive village supports your growth and it may or may not be family. However, they genuinely love and want the best for you. They provide accountability, support and hold you up. They support you, even when you may not be able to stand on your own.

If you don't have a village, you can build one through a support group, church organization and a positive social media group. God can also build you up when you connect with like-minded people that build you and support your growth.

Some people think when you are healed, it is a one-and-done event. This is not always the case. For some, it is going to be a process just like the imposter syndrome: "Imposter syndrome is the experience of feeling like a phony—you feel as though at any moment you are going to be found out as a fraud—like you don't belong where you are and you only got there through chance. It can affect anyone no matter their social status, work background, skill level, or degree of expertise". **Imposter Syndrome: Definition, Symptoms, Traits, Causes and Coping (verywellmind.com)**

Imposter syndrome may come upon occasions. However, you must be intentional to resist self-sabotage. The imposter syndrome will try to come. When it does, you must speak affirmations and encourage yourself as David did. Being in the power of God can be extremely helpful and transformational. Some people think you always need a mentor to be able to significantly heal and become successful.

They believe a professional mentor with a title is necessary for your life to truly transform. However, they may not have realized that you may already have a mentor in a few people within your circle.

This is a prime example that sometimes you can glean from a mentor who doesn't even know they are your mentor. So glean from the seeds of the people around you and take note. I was telling her that I also have friends I glean from. Therefore, you don't just need one person to fit the mentor concept. Different people meet different outcomes. There are times you may need some spiritual, therapeutic, or a combination of both for assistance for deep-seated issues.

You may need intervention for trauma where it's beyond the mentor's role. Therapy can help you to come to where God wants you to be. You want to connect with the right therapist and interview them. If it's not a good fit at the first appointment, move on. Then do some research on what kind of therapist is for you.

You may want a therapist (for example, a therapist specializing in abuse, eating disorders, or addictions) specific to your trauma. It is critical that you find the most appropriate therapist and/or spiritual support. You don't want to give too much information to the wrong therapist. They may not be able to know what to do with the information you have poured out.

This can bring unintended harm to you. There are strategies that the therapist who is right for you is equipped with.

The right therapist or spiritual support will be capable to assist in positioning you where God wants you to be. Licensed therapy may not be for you. Seeking support from your church, local cultural center or support group may also be an option.

A young lady shared she felt rejection when a family member was not there for her when she needed them. I let her know - never put your faith 100% in man. At times, they may not be functioning in the capacity they should. However, pray and love them and accept them.

Life is a process. Life can often be compared to the metamorphosis of a butterfly (https://ansp.org/exhibits/online-exhibits/butterflies/lifecycle/). The beginning process can be gross and difficult. In the beginning, it is hard to see how an ugly centipede can evolve into something beautiful. The middle stages are even more gross and difficult. They have to hang in a sack and be in a vulnerable state and risk death to blossom into who they were destined to be (the butterfly).

During these times, even now, your 100% trust should be in the Lord. With God, nothing is impossible. He will lead you through the metamorphosis process blueprint. This blueprint is the road to holistic health.

Chapter 1: Unique

Get out of self. Reach out and connect with someone because your life is bigger than you. It's a blessing to be a blessing!

When I was age eight, I was in class with a young lady who was special needs. I was drawn to the isolated kids who were bullied, so I had a heart for this young lady. I supported her. It hurt me to see her rejected and isolated and bullied. Her not having anyone compelled me to have compassion for her.

Her special needs made her stand out and people treated her differently and sometimes ignored and isolated her. She didn't fit in with what her peers considered as normal. She was unable to fit in with her classmates and she didn't have any friends. She changed how she interacted with classmates and teachers. Being around me allowed others to connect with her and acknowledge the value in her. It was not anything special about me. It could have been anyone. She needed someone who cared and supported her. I was that someone.

I ended up befriending her mom too and it changed who she was for the better. Everyone is born with a desire to belong and connect with something. She began to feel more confident in who she was. She then began to get the courage to go out and play. She began to feel connected to classmates.

Although she still had to deal with bullies, something in her changed. She no longer suffered from special education rejection. Now she had someone who was an advocate and defended her, which was me. She stayed in school and graduated.

This displays why it is so critical for those of us in a position to serve and advocate for the marginalized, isolated and vulnerable. Your voice and action can change someone's trajectory in life and it may save someone's life.

I became friends with another young lady who was bullied when I moved from Saint Paul to North Minneapolis. People mistreated her. I was around 12 years old and her mom was dealing with her own challenges and overdisciplined her daughter.

Her mom didn't discipline her with the intent of hurting her but with trying to save her. If discipline is not done with love, it may cause more harm than good. Her mom was always disciplining her and my friend stayed on a punishment. I'm not sure if my friend learned anything from her punishment. There were not that many conversations.

I want to be clear here, this did not make her mom a bad person. She was doing what she knew, what she was raised with and what she was equipped for. When she did get out, she had neighborhood friends trying to attack her. She told me she didn't expect me to be her friend.

I was drawn to her as she was someone who was isolated and detached from being social. Her home life was not healthy and I ended up being there for her and supporting her.

After our friendship grew, her self-esteem increased. How she interacted with people changed and her confidence improved. She began to keep up her appearance. Melanie took a wrong turn later in life. She was still facing some self-esteem and self-perception challenges. I never wrote her off. I remained supportive and non-judgmental.

There were times I could not be there for her consistently due to my own family responsibilities and commitments. However, I still made sure to check in or provide her with any knowledge that I was aware of for any resources or support.

I love being connected to the community. And scripture supports the community. It is always important to be connected to a community. Your community may be a church, a support group, an organization, or a club. There can be various avenues of opportunities for potential communities.

It's not for me to define your community. Some people think it has to be a well- known public group. It does not have to be. It all depends on what is for you and what God has for you. However, sometimes people isolate themselves because of trauma, judgment and miscommunication.

There is an excellent movie that talks about the rejection and negative self-talk that can lead to depression. Negative self-talk and self-sabotage are not for your good. Overcoming negative self-talk and depression is imperative to where God wants to take you: it is a process. We must trust the process.

Breaking bad habits is a process, just like breaking the habit of diet coke. I like diet coke and have been working on cutting back. There are times when I replace diet coke with lemon water and seltzer. Some days I may drink more than I should. We have to celebrate the progress even if we go from five a day to two a day until we are completely done with drinking it. *The Bible says* **Though a just man falls seven times, he gets back up with the right mind Proverbs 24:16.** Show yourself grace because we can be our own worst critic and worst enemy.

It's also critical that we renew our minds daily. It is also critical we watch what we hear, see and expose ourselves to. What we take in can break down our self-esteem, self-worth and confidence.

We will start thinking about what we don't have: we should have more clothes, money, friends, parties, etc. We then will get caught up in comparison. We can appreciate how others are doing. But we need to look within ourselves for our worth and value and not the superficial things in life. You can renew your mind with the word of God and positive affirmations.

Romans 12:2
New International Version
> *[2] Do not conform to the pattern of this world but be transformed by the renewing of your mind. Then you will be able to test and approve what God's will is—his good, pleasing and perfect will.*

Chapter 2: His Image

There is no one on the planet like you and you are unique and one of a kind. You are fearfully and wonderfully made and don't let anyone tell you anything different!

Once people radiate and embrace who they really are they will become more accepting of themselves. This accomplishment requires enduring a process. Once the process is complete, you will see (in yourself) someone rare, unique and beautiful. You will understand that no one else is like you or has your fingerprints. Then you begin walking into what God has for you, not the media's view of you.

Those who are not media conscious do not fit in society. They were made to be set apart and gravitate to what God has for them. Not to say social media is taboo. However, there must be a balance. Social media can be both helpful and harmful. Everybody has a specific purpose. We are all born with a specific purpose.

Before you were created in your mother's womb, you were God-created for your purpose. He set that purpose up before each one of us was born. Therefore, we are exactly where we need to be no matter what we have been through.

No matter what we experienced and endured: rejection, abandonment, abuse, divorce, the wrong choices or prosecution. We are not damaged goods because Christ is the healer. God shows us grace. Some people may not have ever been through anything. However, there are people that have been through something who need to hear your story.

God has adorned us for all the greatness that cannot be minimized. If we are not careful, we can share our story with the wrong individual. In doing so, people can get prideful and thorny and discount our story. Your story is not meant for everyone. A woman shared with me she was listening to a popular social media influencer who has many followers and who puts people down. A lot of individuals who have been through trauma are drawn to this individual's broadcast.

This social media personality fragments the truth into half-truths or lies. As these fans call into the broadcast, this person tears them down, sizes them up, and then rips them apart. This person tells them they are mediocre. Also, anyone that calls into this person's show they don't allow them to speak.

This influencer preys on traumatized individuals. Be careful of who influences you and remember they are human and have flaws as we all do. No one is perfect. No matter what they are trying to present. Their word is not bond. Always remember to eat the meat and throw out the bones.

No one should make someone like that their God! This individual likes to target people. It's okay to follow social media influencers, but do it with awareness and guidance.

We have the blueprint, the word of God. God uses tools such as books to guide us and a primary guidebook is the word of God. God provides us with directions and guidelines. We can find some of those strategies and tools through his word. We must make sure we are equipping ourselves and speak life to ourselves and others. Our words have power.

We need to be diligent and purposeful and come into agreement with God's blueprint. I lived through trauma and experienced relationships in my past that were familiar with my trauma that destroyed my self-esteem. However, the love of God continues to strengthen and build me into the woman He created me to be.

There are also tools out there that help to restore the soul from trauma. Now I know how this world can give you the message that you don't deserve to be here. The world can convince you that you don't fit in and that you don't qualify. The world will tell you that you are not the right size, race, class, culture, or complexion.

Society has a way of making you feel like you don't measure up, you're not worthy, or that you are a reject. Whether rejection comes from various groups, friends, enemies, or even family, it impacts your self-esteem. Yes, it can get that real. It's happened to those close to me; and yes, even me.

When you are born with the spirit of rejection, you can carry that for years. But I'm here to say that it no longer has to be a part of your life. However, overcoming rejection may be a process.

I knew a young lady who needed help dealing with her abusive partner. The young man (her child's father) was hostile. The way he came after her was threatening. The situation became so dangerous that law enforcement had to be called. These police officers were specifically trained in mental health and were trained in the area of de-escalation.

I want to be clear that if you know of any committed, stable individuals with guidance capabilities in this area (de-escalation), try this intervention first if you can. I asked her why she was still with him. She said her mom died early and her first child's dad was severely abusive. She said she tried to walk (leave him), but she couldn't because she was homeless. She needed help and so did her partner.

I spoke to this young lady's potential, humanity and saw her beyond her current condition. I met her where she was. I asked her what her dreams and goals for herself and her family were. I assisted her with mapping out her plans and breaking down her goals into small steps.

I met with her to create small incremental goals. With each small goal, she made she felt empowered. She started to look better as she visited. At first, she looked bad but then started to better care for herself. Others did not understand why I was taking time with her and giving her extra time. However, because I was able to sit and listen, she began to open up.

I was able to hear her story and began to acknowledge her and she felt better. She became more comfortable and confident, independent and strong. As a result, she was also more self-assured and felt better about herself. This was empowering because other avenues of people were not listening to her. I also referred her significant other to receive support, guidance and direction from an agency that could assist him.

Sometimes I would take a break with her. However, I would soon resume intervention because I am a woman of my word. It was important to her that I would always get back to her. Even if I did not have a solution at that moment, it made a difference to her. I have watched her evolve and change. She has genuinely experienced positive growth. She finally left the relationship with the young man and she began to pursue a lot of her dreams and goals. She began to change some of her unhealthy desires and behaviors.

Her story has been heard. More stories like hers need to be heard. People need to know that this type of transformation can really happen. I am familiar with these types of situations because I have lived them and I was her in a period of my early life. It's really just the enemy who is trying to set ablaze the fire and sometimes he will work overtime. Because you are a trailblazer and are different, be prepared to face isolation and persecution.

Different is not what everybody agrees with. Different is not status quo or formal. When you come on the scene, they haven't seen this before and it's okay. Your style may be knew to them but continue to be who you are. Hearing other's stories that no one wants to hear is a representation of the Compassion of Christ.

Even now, I have people that tell me I have something to offer. I didn't always believe that. How could someone like me have something to offer? Some see me as a system changer and one who empowers. I see myself as someone different who is willing to share some of her lived experiences. The young lady I mentioned earlier also shared with me that sometimes I have played a strategist mentor to her.

You may be the one God is using to break up the familiar behavior, attitudes and challenge the behavior of others. I learned to trust God. He has shown me how to be confident in him. God is using me. Be not dismayed because God has you and all of heaven is backing you. You must trust that self-sabotage should be treated like an enemy that you have zero tolerance for.

You may have to challenge people that do not want to be challenged. And those self-sabotaging voices can be discouraging. When these voices come, pray and seek God. Get affirmed about who God created you to be and your purpose.

The beginning of this chapter talks about being fearfully and wonderfully made. When we think of something fearfully and wonderfully made, one creature that comes to mind is the butterfly. The butterfly is so beautiful. However, there was a necessary process that resulted in that beauty. It did not happen overnight. Their process started off ugly, rigid and fearful. They begin in isolation and in the dark. We can relate our transformation process to that of the butterfly.

The butterfly develops through a process called metamorphosis. Metamorphosis is a Greek word meaning transformation or change in shape. There are four stages of transformation for the butterfly. These four stages are the egg, larva, pupa and adult.

During the egg stage, they are hatched and laid on plants. These plants are the egg's food. The egg develops into caterpillars or vulva. The caterpillar is the feeding stage. The caterpillar needs as much food as it can get. The high food intake is so it can grow to its biggest or potential size (ansp.org/exhibits/online-exhibits/butterflies/lifecycle).

The food during the caterpillar stage is also stored for adulthood. During this time, it splits its skin. The caterpillar then sheds skin about four or five times. The pupa or second stage is one of the most critical stages. When the caterpillar is full-grown, he stops eating and becomes a pupa.

Some pupa are suspended under a branch or hidden by leaves or hidden underground. Often times when we are in transition, we are hidden or feel like we are in a wilderness stage but it is necessary for our protection or the preservation of our destiny.

I remember Pastor and Movie Producer Devon Franklin sharing a story about the butterfly. Devon Franklin shared that someone once saw a pupa inside a cocoon of silk hanging off under a branch. The person decided to help the butterfly. The person decided to get the butterfly out of its uncomfortable hidden cocoon. As a result, the butterfly died!

Often times when we are in our wilderness situation, it seems too painful. We feel like we need someone to rescue us. Depending on who we are around (and should not be around), they can potentially rescue us from the pain of the process. However, their rescue could abort our "necessary" process and by default, abort our mission.

The adult stage of the butterfly is the reproductive stage. Just like the butterfly, we experience the reproductive stage in adulthood as well. However, just like the butterfly, during childhood, our job is to attain nutrition for development and survival. Many people do not understand what we go through as children. Many people do not understand that a lot of trauma can be experienced in childhood.

Often times the pain of childhood can make us feel like we were adults. I can remember times when I thought I couldn't wait to grow up so I wouldn't have to deal with whatever trauma I was experiencing. However, children who grow up too fast struggle in some areas of maturity in their adulthood. We need to experience the fullness of each stage of our lives so that we can "holistically" develop and thrive at each different stage of our life.

The caterpillar stage can be compared to our adolescent and teenage stage. During this time we are in the middle of growth. Just like the caterpillar we are not quite at the age of adulthood but have graduated from the underdeveloped childhood stage. However, we are still in a stage where we must receive nutrients to maximize our growth potential.

During the caterpillar stage, there can be many challenges. You are in between and not quite where you may want to be. You are looking at the pretty butterflies flying, soaring and reproducing. You may be wishing you were there. You must realize that just like the caterpillar, you may be looking at successful people thinking you can't wait or you should be there.

Always remember they were where you are and most of them did not get there overnight. The ones who did get there overnight will not stay at the top too long unless they are willing to be reprocessed.

We must trust the process. One of the most end result rewarding stages is when we are in the trenches and then we fully complete the process! Sometimes the wilderness stage is the loneliest stage. We feel most alone and boxed in.

Just like when the butterfly is in the pupa stage, they are closed in an incubator type of silk cocoon. They have to endure lots of pressure to be completely processed in this stage before they become the beautiful butterfly we see.

Often times we hear people say "They see the Glory but they don't know my story. People may see how anointed, beautiful and productive you are. They do not know the process you had to take. They did not know the pain, the necessary sacrifice it took. However, without the sacrifice and breakthrough, you would not be where you are or where you are trying to go.

The purpose of the butterfly adult stage is to mate and lay eggs. The butterfly lives up to the "be fruitful and multiply and replenish the earth" scrip-ture . We do not want to be ever learning but never able.

When we have received all of the food and knowledge and stored it up for an appointed time for us to reproduce them, we must execute the reproduction phase. God does not give us a calling for us to walk in just to sit and look pretty. The butterfly is indeed pretty. But the butterfly works and reproduces its kind at an accelerated rate. We are to be the same way.

In order to be holistic, we must be complete. That means we must go through every critical phase required for success and complete development: physical, mental, emotional and spiritual.

God has not called you to get multiple degrees, become a millionaire, own a business, attain a prestigious status just to brag about it. You must be willing to lead, empower and attract protégé's you can influence and impact. These protégés should be able to duplicate what you are doing and even in a greater measure.

Just like Jesus says in the Bible: *"He that believeth in me and the works that I do, those shall he do and even greater" John 14:12.*

Most people at first thought Jesus was saying that those that believe him shall be greater in power than him. That is not what Jesus meant. He meant the demonstration of power should be more quantifiable, not more qualitative in power or rank. We must surrender to and trust the process.

Trust God, he knows the end of a thing as well as the beginning. It is in the completion of the process that greatness is revealed. If we endure the process, we will allow the Glory of God to express how fearfully and wonderfully he made us.

Chapter 3: Different

The Gift of Being Different.

Your difference is not a curse but a blessing!

There is a gift in being different. We can be challenged by being different, different size, age, a different background, a different race, or a different whatever. We must be unashamed about being different as we trust God through the process. Your difference is a blessing! Don't get caught up in the hype.

There are many people God has graced to be different. The following are examples of people whose differences have transformed and shaped our society. They did not allow someone to convince them their differences had no meaning. They instead refuse to be distracted, walked through the process with determination. This determination allowed them to avoid being shaped into not maximizing the potential in their differences:

Malcolm X (Different): he believed change should take place by any means necessary.

Gandhi (Different): he believed non-violence would result in justice.

Mother Teresa (Different): she transformed the world by showing us what unconditional love means, living up to the verse God is no respecter of persons. Lizzo (Different): she shifted the body image culture and set the standard that intelligence and success do not require a status quo shape.

Michael J (Different): shattered glass ceilings and was not a conformist and dared to be unpredictable.

Prince (Different): shattered glass ceilings, a creative who built success outside the box.

Steve Jobs (Different): he created an empire at Microsoft

Kamila Harris (Different): shattered gender barriers and leadership barriers creating a leader-shift.

Elon Musk (Different): Created Telsa, took technology and sustainable energy to the next level.

Esther in the Bible: Esther helped save a nation of people, her People, God's People and oppressed people, a kingdom.

Your difference is a blessing! It brings a different perspective, call, anointing, hope and confidence.

Don't doubt the calling on your life. You were born for such a time for this! The difference may mean a break in the normal, tradition or the familiar. It can be scary and cause fear.

Martin Luther King was different, Rosa Parks was different, but they broke the mode of what appeared normal. We now have various (and no longer a one size fits all) types of fashion models, sizes, races, etc. But they all bring their confidence and callings.

Being different can bring us fear. Because of bad experiences and rejection from others, and sometimes others are classmates, associates, friends, and even family.

Trust that God is working behind the scenes for your good and the good of others. Your difference was not just for you but for others. Your difference provides hope, acceptance, love and God's supernatural work at hand.

God is arranging your difference for God's purpose and a bigger plan. This can be difficult in a time like this, a pandemic. We are in a time where social media strongly influences society's views and way of thinking.

We live in a day where society's strand of beauty of what's normal and what's okay is a soundboard for what appears to be acceptable. We are here to show and expedite God's work, orchestration, hope and plan for his Glory.

Matthew 5:16
Let your light so shine before men, that they may see your good works and glorify God
which is in heaven.

Ephesians 2:10
For we are God's masterpiece. He has created us anew in Christ Jesus, so we can do the good things he planned for us long ago.

I admire many of the trailblazers mentioned earlier.

This is because their differences didn't stop or deter

their dreams or goals. I guess you can say my humble

beginnings started off different.

A lot of my experiences were tough. There were lots

of hills and valleys. I was born to two teen parents

who were not ready to be parents. They were still

experiencing life as teenagers and rightly so.

They were trying to cope with life themselves. They had a lot of challenges.

My dad was working a lot of hours and living life. I was not a priority for him at the time. At age ten, he asked me if I wanted to stay with him but I said no because I felt my grandparent's house was a place of safety and structure for me at the time. I also did not understand in detail at the time why my dad wanted me to live with him. But later I realized he wanted to raise and nurture me. But he did not make that clear at the time.

My mom had a lot of traumatic experiences to deal with that impacted her life and her choices. My parents' choices impacted the foundation of my life and some of the choices I made. Their choices impacted my self-esteem, fear of abandonment. I also experienced rejection. However, with God, some work and the healing process, I am healed! I love them dearly and we're in a much better place in our relationships. God has really filled in those gaps in the relationships I had with my parents.

While my parents were still moving around and living, they didn't have me with them. This was also because I was raised by my grandparents until age 12. However, my parents did their best to try and visit me but they were trying to figure out life themselves at the young age they were.

My grandfather was a Pullman porter on Amtrak and he would leave for a week to work. When my grandfather would leave for work my grandma was not healthy and struggled with her mental and chemical health. During that time her language towards me and others in the house became damaging and harmful.

She would call me names and it was the loneliest and scariest experience in my life. When my grandfather would leave, I believe my grandmother experienced fear of abandonment. Her projecting out to me was just a part of her own pain and trauma.

My grandmother did not talk that much about her background. My grandmother was a Baptist who converted to Catholicism for her husband. My grandma didn't practice Christianity but saw it as a religion. She believed in God and reverenced Him but there were no foundational Christian practices in our home at the time. For example, we never went to mass or church except for a funeral or baptism.

In our home, there was a Psalm 23 paper inside of a drawer. I would open the drawer and would read Psalm 23 at age two. Yes, I began to read at age two! That scripture provided me comfort and protection every time I read it.

I would always read Psalms 23 and that was my saving grace. I read Psalm 23 when I felt scared and rejected and did not feel loved. When my grandma would fall, pass out or not be in her sound mind. I didn't know if she would fall and seriously hurt herself. I would cry out to God and ask him for help. Thank God someone would eventually come and help. They would come and help her and get her off the floor.

Once my grandparents' kids were all grown it was just me, my grandmother and my grandfather. My grandparents raised me from a baby to age 12 and took time to nurture me with just me in the house.

I got my aunts and uncles' parents in a way they didn't. So there was rejection I experienced on multiple levels from my aunts and uncles as well. This was because (my grandparents had 13 kids) my aunts and uncles felt they (my grandparents) did not pay them the attention that I received.

There were times my mom would try to come to get us (my brother and I) but would take us back to our grandparents. When my grandfather had cancer I had to move with my mom. My mom had two older sisters that started taking care of my grandmother when my grandad got sick. They were mean to me and passively-aggressively showed it by pushing me into walls and dropping food on me.

They also said things to me you should not say to a child. They were twin sisters. They told me why they did not like me after my grandmother died. Why they didn't like me made sense. It also demonstrates how their emotional and mental trauma impacted them and others. I got the special attention from their parents they did not receive and they were still hurt.

My grandparents had all these kids back to back and they took time and raised me. As a result, their children were rejected. This shows how unforgiveness robs people of their sanity and mental health. Grown children can be mad at their parents.

Please take note, they (my grandparents) were parents in a time where they lived through segregation. And again, my grandmother was Catholic so she felt she had to have 13 kids. I have a lot of grace for my aunts and uncles now as I see what they had to go through. I no longer look at them with lenses of detriment but mercy. It showed me how I show grace to my offenders and others and how I didn't want to be bitter and have animosity toward my mom and dad.

I also understand my dad was abandoned by his mom and had to live with his dad and grew up at a young age. He had his own job and had his own apartment at 15. He stayed in contact with me and I knew he was my dad.

As my grandmother's health deteriorated I would try and see my grandmother when my aunts cared for her before she died. My aunts would not let me in the house and she died a year and a half after my grandfather. The doctors had no diagnosis for her death. Her organs were shutting down but there was no diagnosis for it. It was like a failure to thrive. I think her death was due to a broken heart.

Before she died she spoke to me as a young woman. My grandmother spoke to my future. She looked at me in the eye and she said "Nichol, you are going to do great things and you are going to be an incredible woman". My grandmother never talked to me like that before. It was very prophetic!

Chapter 4: Fear

Fear may show its ugly head at times but press forward and use the energy of the anxiety as fuel to take you to the next level.

Fear can be crippling and paralyzing, especially if you came from an environment that instilled fear in you, whether it was abandonment, abuse, rejection, or experiences. Those situations can leave lasting imprints that can keep us frozen in time.

We all have heard that fear is false evidence appearing real. But it is so true; it is not real! 2: Timothy 1:7 states that **God has not given us the spirit of fear, but of power and love and of a sound mind.**

I had some resentment towards my mom, because of her life choices. She was living a fast life. She was making unhealthy decisions and choices. I felt the streets were chosen over me so there was resentment. There was also a short time my brother and I were in foster care.

After the short foster care experience, we went back with my grandparents for a short period. I was grateful to go back to my grandparents. I felt loved and nurtured.

I moved with my mom to the Northside of Minneapolis when my Grandparents died. The Northside is where there was deep poverty. Neighbors were asking for food and there was lots of crime and I was being bullied. It was like I got dropped in an environment and I had to adjust quickly. I had come to realize my Grandparents sheltered and protected me.

I was so different. I experienced intense rejection. I was being rejected by some people who are saying, why are you here? You don't talk like us and you don't belong. It was a challenging period in my life and I had to pass multiple life tests.

I now appreciate my journey and it helped develop me into the strong and resilient woman I am. I love North Minneapolis and the beauty and community that it has to offer, despite the disparities that it's been challenged with. There are beautiful people there and many great people have come from there and still do until this day.

The transition from the Rondo Saint Paul neighborhood with excellent grades to the Northside was drastic and scary. That transition from Saint Paul to the Northside was when my grades plummeted. There was a teacher who pushed me and would not let me quit when I wanted to. I did well because of her.

There were a lot of struggles in the neighborhood and my mom was in an abusive relationship. I was terrified of her boyfriend. Although there was poverty in some of the neighborhoods, my mom always kept a clean home and sometimes we had roaches no matter how spotless our home was. I would babysit for neighbors in our building and they would leave me with their kids. I would have to find food for the kids because their parents left me with their kids for hours with no food. You talk about stressed; I was. This was especially when I looked at their little faces.

Mom suffered from abusive relationships. This traumatized my brother - he is fine now. My mom's boyfriend was talking to me as if he wanted me to do what he wanted me to do and I was scared.

That was when I met my friend in this neighborhood. I joined a drum core drill team and it was my saving grace. In the drill team, I would dance and found a community of people I connected with. We used to march and dance. I was 12 when I met my first boyfriend (in this drill team community). He initially supported me and was someone to talk to about my life, family and challenges.

Things were bad at home and my mom's boyfriend would hit us physically and was abusive to the females in the home. My mom's boyfriend would nit-pick about little stuff.

Because my mom's boyfriend began to hit me and I didn't feel safe and wanted to leave. I connected with a lady in the neighborhood and she was a young mother with two small children. I moved and stayed with her and we lived through the worst and the best of the times. Sometimes the struggle was very real.

She opened her very tiny apartment to me and I was able to stay in school and continue with my studies. I ended up having a child at fifteen years old. I quickly was thrown into a major responsibility of another life. It was challenging and a wake-up call. But I know that every child is a gift no matter the circumstances.

Those years were full of ups and downs and I worked, studied and parented. And I ultimately graduated from high school! I was also in survivor mode, dealing on the level I was equipped and experienced pain, abandonment, rejection and judgment. Those years I was barely making it and existing through life. I had some tough experiences, but I made it and God was with me.

I thank God for the angels I met on my journey: a social worker, a supportive teacher, a kind co-worker and a woman's advocate. I'm grateful for these people because they didn't have to reach out and connect for my sheer survival at times.

I lived and continued for a purpose and God's divine orchestration. To Glory and Good! Forgiveness, healing, and growth will allow you to continue with life, live your best life, and trust God with your entire journey.

Use that anxiety and fear to motivate and propel you to your challenge, goal and overcome obstacles. Obstacles are placed in our lives for us to overcome them. Obstacles are designed to build us and propel us to greater. Take the leap over faith to navigate you to your destiny and where God wants you to go.

This is the time to rise above your fears. Doing so will always take you higher. Your challenge to overcome fear will build you into a stronger, more competent and resilient person.

So what if someone says no, you have a negative critic, stutter through a speech, and get denied a job opportunity or a business deal. It only means you're closer to your outcome, goal and finish line. Listen to the still voice of God and trust He is guiding you there.

Chapter 5: Grace

Forgiveness and Grace will release the chain of bondage and set you on course for a life full of growth and love.

Forgiveness is critical for growth and not forgiving can keep you bound, stagnant and in a stronghold. In life, we are going to experience tough times, offenses and betrayal. Some of these experiences may be from close family members, friends, associates or strangers.

These experiences can also come from even us. We don't want to be tied to those situations. This kind of tie is no good for our growth and purpose in this life.

It can chip away at your self-esteem and happiness. Forgiveness is more for you than anyone else. We reside and take up space in an imperfect world and with imperfect people. God has called us to forgive because he forgives us. He would not ask us to do something that we are not equipped to do.

I have witnessed how impactful forgiveness is. I have also witnessed the negative effects of unforgiveness. It can cause bitterness, depression, anger and anxiety. It can also lock entire families and communities into strongholds. This will cause them to lose out on love, growth and blessings. Not forgiving closes doors to joy, peace, possibilities and all that the Lord has for us.

I also want to be clear that some people you forgive may no longer be living. Some of them are living but may never apologize. They may be a toxic person or you may never have contact with them again in your life. You don't have to have them present if that is not healthy or possible.

Release the pain, hurt, rejection and offense. Forgive yourself, them and let it go. Cancel the debt as God prefers us not to remain in resentment. The price tag is too expensive and too costly. Move on to freedom, forgiveness and God's love so he can open new doors of elevation. Forgiveness may not be letting someone back in your life if they are toxic. If you let them back in, you may have to reposition them with boundaries.

God truly orchestrated my steps when I went back to school and got my associate's degree. I'm glad to have gone to the school I went to. The school gave me direction and focus along my higher educational journey. I felt like that was a real turnaround. Part of the turnaround began when I got saved and filled with the Holy Spirit.

There were shackles that fell off from the trauma I carried. I felt those weights fall off. I was 31 when I went up (to the church alter) for prayer one day. The Pastor said "Forgive your offender. You have to forgive him. I want you to open your mouth and say it." I started choking and coughing!

The Pastor told me to pray for the next few days and call that person when I say it. Tell them you forgive them and they will forgive you. When I did what the Pastor instructed, I felt burdens lifted. I felt light as a feather!

When I did call my accuser and spoke with them, we were able to have a conversation. There was a breakthrough for both of us that brought some healing and closure. I believed it helped us to be able to move on in our lives.

Some people don't get over the offense. They stay bitter forever. I'm thankful I let it go as I wouldn't have the blessings I have now. God and the Holy Spirit are now able to reign in my heart due to forgiveness.

All the things I wanted people to say to me; like "please forgive me" and that they would be so sorry and come to me have not happened. However, you must do your part in the matter.

Forgiveness is for you. God has taught me not to wait for them to say it. I may be 80 years old when they decide to do so! Some may never choose to say it to you.

There are people literally waiting for people to come and say sorry. Some offenders don't get it and we don't and can't wait for that forgiveness. Again as stated earlier, forgiveness is for us. God equips us to forgive. We are equipped to forgive and that's our job to forgive.

I watch people bound in offense and it keeps families in a stronghold of bondage. God does not want us to do that. You cannot carry that generational curse around. You can forgive people that are not in your life or those that are still in your sphere. Remember, we didn't always know what we know now, so give others grace when they don't have it all figured out. God gives us grace and mercy and he models that so we can pay it forward to others.

My walk with God was well but the relationship with people had been shaky. "How did you become so connected to God?" Many people ask me. I began to seek God for myself and experience intimacy with him. There would be times I would have a Holy Spirit experience.

The word of God was my saving grace and I read and meditated on the word intensely. I kept reading over and over what God promised me until His word became real and evident in my life. Confessing the word has the power to transform your atmosphere, environment and situation.

It would be just me and God and it was intense. It was a love session with God in an intimate spiritual type of way. When I was pregnant with my second son I had a mentor I worked with. She was very spiritual.

She had a strong mothering spirit. She (along with the word of God) was my saving grace during a difficult time in my life.

Chapter 6: Wellness

Wellness is precious and priceless.

If anything has reminded us just how important wellness is, it's the COVID-19 Pandemic. Suddenly, our world was turned upside down. Some of us have experienced the loss of loved ones, social isolation, limited connections, job loss and loss of support.

The messaging from the media daily was on Covid-19 daily deaths. The media inundated us with underlying conditions of higher risk factors for certain people. Many started focusing on their holistic health mentally, emotionally, physically and spiritually. Holistic health became a priority while also trying to cope with our new reality.

Our overall wellness has to be a priority. Our bodies are the temple of the Holy Spirit. What we do with it and how we nurture and care for it, will impact how we move, function, survive and thrive in this world.

We don't have to be wellness experts, we must take out time daily to schedule in what is important. Prayer, mediation, walks and workouts are critical as well as being cautious of what we hear, see, eat and accept in our space.

We also have to schedule our medical appointments with providers for preventive care. Do I like to do these things? No! But I do it because I want to have quality and quantity of life so I can be there to serve for family and community. I want to make the most of my days and be impactful for God's Glory and Purpose. It's all about balance, so read up on health, holistic and cultural methods. So, we can be our best selves and live our best lives.

Reduce social media, news media, read the word (Bible) and read books for your personal development. It's all a journey, I'm not where I want to be, but I'm making progress and modeling that for my loved ones.

Chapter 7: Reset

You can RESET and REINVENT Your life at any time. We are all here for a divine purpose and adapting is a part of the process.

We can always start over and reinvent ourselves no matter where we are in our lives or what age we are. While we are here in this life and breathing, we have a purpose. Our purpose may change and shift.

You don't have to stay stuck - you can shift, reinvent and reset. Regardless of what I experienced in my life and the unthinkable insurmountable challenges, God was able to reset my life for purpose, profession and for His Glory.

Through all those trials and tribulations it allowed me to have grace. It also allowed me to be able to advocate for people in those same circumstances. It reminded me of how Jesus was not supported and he ended up with only three of the 12 Apostles staying with him.

It's amazing how he was rejected and persecuted. And just like Jesus, I walked it out literally. I had to "walk it out" although my journey was a different path than Christ. God will anoint your head with oil and make a table before you in the presence of your enemies.

There are people you have in your life when you want to quit that encourage you. That is why I am so passionate about Human Services. I believe in paying it forward. This has been my life and legacy.

What sparked the calling to Human Services started in sixth- grade. I was in 6th grade when I befriended another friend. All kids need is one person to make a positive influence to inspire and help them transform their lives. I feel like God would always send angels to protect and surround me and care for me. Just like my friend named Linda. She became my children's godmother *and she was God-Sent.*

There was a social worker in high school that was very helpful. I was pregnant with my first son. She told me to meet with her. She told me there would be a program for students with children who do not go to the school. During this time I had to stay with my friend Linda. I lived between her and a friend's house and a cousin's house. I was couch hopping but still went to high school.

I also had a part-time job. The Social Worker still advocated for me to stay in school. The Social Worker helped me focus on positive influences and goal setting. Because of her, I was able to focus and tune out the distractions.

I never had a relationship with God at first because there was hypocrisy. I saw with some of the people who attended the church. I witnessed this hypocrisy and was fearful and scared. I would see a popular minister on television and I would be scared!

When I would go out on the weekend I felt like I no longer belonged there. Some people were not saved telling me I was not supposed to be there. I felt like I was in a dark place and then God begun to pull on me. A lot of people think I have been saved forever. I have not been saved forever. I believe it is the grace of God on my life where He makes all things new as if you never sinned!

This faith journey is a process. What keeps me is, when a person falls I am not there to condemn them. I yield to my power in God and rely on Him as my cup could run empty. The best thing to do in that situation is to always pray and seek wisdom and direction from

God. What also keeps me is being gracious to others because I am in need of grace.

We should love as God loves. You don't keep a record of other's wrongs. You are merciful and compassionate on the least just as God is compassionate to you. There is an unnecessary disconnect when people come into the church with addiction issues and infirmities we should dare not look down on them.

There was a lady who came into a church I was a member of. She asked for help and confessed she had issues. No one wanted to get involved or help her. I could not really help her. No one knew what to do with her. They were scared of her and were judging her and she eventually left. It was like we are ministering and helping people but because we lack a lot of compassion, a lot of people are turned away.

Some institutions are disconnected from the cultures of the day. However, there are some ministries doing incredible work. From a child, I have grown to have compassion for people. I know what it's like to be rejected and bullied and abused. I know how painful that was for me so my heart is drawn to people like that.

Rejection is a spirit. You can walk around with the spirit of rejection. If the Lord accepts you, the rejection is no longer your portion. You don't have to carry that mantle. You no longer have to walk in rejection and self-pity. That comes from the enemy.

The enemy knows how to get people at an early age feeling rejected. This is so he can infiltrate a spirit of rejection.

My associates and bachelor's degrees are in Human Services. I also have a Master's in Human Services with a focus on Family Studies. I have done it and yes, it was a little scary. However, what were my options? Not to move, not to grow and just exist? Certainly not!

I'll never forget deciding to return to college at 40. My mind was telling me I was too old. I began to believe that I wouldn't be able to learn new information and technology. I began to convince myself to just follow the status quo.

I'm glad I didn't listen to the voices in my mind. I jumped out on faith and did it! It was the best thing I have ever done. I met so many wonderful people, learned so much information and it changed my world both personally and professionally. I shudder at thinking of the outcome if I had not returned to school. Now my personal and professional experiences have equipped me with the credibility and competency to help mediate and advocate for individuals and communities.

I was also able to reset when it came to my life as a widow. This was after my first husband passed from cancer. I could have stayed in grief. But I renewed my mind with the word of God and began to live. Through God's orchestration, love and marriage found its way back into my life!

I want to give hope to anyone. If it is love, a business, criminal background, bankruptcy, reconciliation or whatever you want to start, do it! I encourage you to jump out on faith and start new. You won't regret it. Good things come with Reinvention and Resetting! We have so many examples: Saul to Paul, Joseph, Esther, Michelle Obama, etc.

Everyone desires a sense of belonging. Until I was reunified with my family I had a longing be reconnected to my family. There are seasons in relationships. There is a saying: "people come into your life for a reason and a season and the time in certain relationships fill its purpose." Sometimes that season is up.

When the season ends, one of the people in the relationship ends it (the relationship). At times that person (who ended the relationship) feels obligated to continue the relationship. They should not feel this way. There are friends I have now that I love but we are not currently connected on a regular basis. That is okay.

Chapter 8: Serve

Serve others and pay it forward. You will be a blessing and it will build you and cultivate you for greatness.

We were placed in this world to serve and to be of service. God did not just put us on this earth for ourselves, no matter our occupations, position, or place in this life. We don't have to be wealthy or to be of significant status.

We exist for others, family and God. To be of service brings personal growth and development. It also builds our community to improve and create healthy environments. Whether it's volunteering to tutor, assisting at a battered women's shelter, your presence can make an impact!

Even if it's an animal shelter, neighborhood board, committee, or homeless program, just volunteer. If you can't give your time, give money, but do something.

Every blessed person I know donates, volunteers, or serves their church or community somewhere. Even if you have a background issue or have been incarcerated, still serve. Someone needs to hear your story.

Maybe it's young people at risk of going down the wrong road who need you. Your story may be what they need to hear to intervene. Maybe you're a single mother. Babysit for another mother. We all have a purpose to serve. We have to come out of ourselves because what we are here for is bigger than us.

Being of service opens us up to God's presence, miracles and growth in our gifts. A servant mindset also propels us into stronger discernment, increased faith and joy. Being of service also brings great joy and peace. Try it, because you will have nothing to lose and will only gain.

1 Peter 4:10 tells us, **as each has received a gift, use it to serve one another, as good stewards of God's varied grace.**

Chapter 9: Legacy

Legacy
Merriam-Webster definition 2: Legacy: Something transmitted by or received from an ancestor or predecessor or from the past.

Sometimes we hear the word legacy and may think about how it applies to us. We often believe legacy is simply money and tangibles. Some of it is that, but much of it is spiritual legacy. God wants us to create a spiritual legacy to lead.

We must pour in and leave a spiritual legacy for our loved ones and others. A spiritual legacy is a guide to pursuing identity, purpose and destiny. God wants us to influence others in loving and positive ways.

Through wisdom, knowledge, prayer, education and role modeling, we can build a legacy. Money can also be a means to build a legacy. Time is so important; and of the essence. Living in our Godly purpose is the foundation of our legacy (and living by the word of God). Living in our Godly purpose also involves living it out in the presence of our loved ones, family, community and the world.

You have the power to plant your seeds of legacy even through brief or temporary interactions. Leave a lasting imprint of God's love on others' lives. Queen Esther's Obedience freed a nation (of her people).

Martin Luther King left a legacy that we benefit from today. The Peaceful Protests have helped provide equity for those who were equity deprived in past times.

Our grandparents endured so that our parents, we, and children can benefit from their legacies of sacrifice. Grab the Paton and pass it on for even GREATER!!

Don't hold on to whatever is blocking your legacy development. Release and Rise!!! People create a legacy for their family, community and children. By building legacy, we also break generational curses. God will send people in your life to plant seeds and use them to impact your family.

The Bible is full of examples demonstrating people who didn't come from the best circumstances. Look at Jesus and David. When God takes you higher He will broaden your audience. Share some of your experiences and let it set someone free to continue a legacy of freedom and empowerment.

You are writing your story now and there are chapters still left to write. God will expand your territory and take you to places of transformational leadership. People, families, lives and organizations are waiting for your blueprint and story

Conclusion

We are currently in trying times. However, you must remind yourself that you were divinely created for such a time as this. You must trust the fact that God would not give you more than you can handle. He provides us with all the tools and the promises to endure and overcome.

Most of us have experienced trauma and hurt in one way or another. We just have to remind ourselves to heal, grow and elevate. We can be impacted by the imposter syndrome that we don't belong, we are not good enough or don't measure up. Don't believe the lies. God puts everything in us so that we are worthy, valuable and priceless. We are created to build, be creative and to belong to something bigger than us for God's Glory. There is greatness in your DNA and so that means you have a destiny and a purpose.

We need to walk in forgiveness and grace for ourselves and others so that we don't become stuck. Forgiveness allows you to experience, in the proper time and season, a smooth reset. It is time to Reset, Revive, Relearn and Rebuild for a better, happier and more joyful life.

As we access how challenging life can be at different times and through different experiences, I have come to know and realize that offenses, life and failures may knock us down. But it does not have to keep us down if we have the awareness that those times were not to destroy us. We must never forget those times that were intended to build us into the conquerors that God created to us be.

"John 16:33, KJV. "Ye are of God, little children and have overcome them: because greater is he that is in you, than he that is in the world."

Go forth in life despite opposition. Push through the storms and disappointments. Those roadblocks are building you for your purpose and greatness! You are leaving a legacy of rich overcoming stories, resilience and God's guidance and hand on your life.

You are leaving directions for others. This is your testimony and blueprint for others. This blueprint will show how you did it. It will provide a *holistic* blueprint for them. This holistic overcomer blueprint will empower them and guide them on how to survive and thrive!

Reflections and Thoughts

www.ingramcontent.com/pod-product-compliance
Lightning Source LLC
Chambersburg PA
CBHW071009160426
43193CB00012B/1984